BUILDING RESILIENCE

T5-CQR-700

Building Confidence

HONOR HEAD

CRABTREE
PUBLISHING COMPANY
WWW.CRABTREEBOOKS.COM

www.crabtreebooks.com

Published in Canada
Crabtree Publishing
616 Welland Ave.
St. Catharines, Ontario
L2M 5V6

Published in the United States
Crabtree Publishing
347 Fifth Avenue
Suite 1402–145
New York, NY 10016

Published in 2021 by Crabtree Publishing Company

First published in Great Britain in 2020
by The Watts Publishing Group
Copyright © The Watts Publishing Group, 2020

Author: Honor Head

Editorial director: Kathy Middleton

Editors: Amy Pimperton, Ellen Rodger

Proofreader: Melissa Boyce

Designers: Peter Scoulding and Cathryn Gilbert

Cover design: Peter Scoulding

**Production coordinator
and Prepress technician:** Tammy McGarr

Print coordinator: Katherine Berti

Consultant: Clare Arnold, psychotherapist and child and adolescent mental health services professional

Printed in the U.S.A./012021/CG20201102

Picture credits
Shutterstock: Nate Allred 7b; Anouki 17c, 30c; BMJ 5tr; Blanscape 11b; Tatyana Bolotova 22b; Edwin Butter 2, 8t; Mircea Costina 27tr; Gorken Demir front cover, title page; Deny 21c; fantom_rd 7t; Florida stock 22t; Giedriius 19c; Dmitrii Golubev 24b; Pascale Gueret 23cl; Mario_ Hoppmann 13b; Issumi1 11t, 30b; Kamonrat 13t; KarlDesign 29b; Heiko Kiera 21t; Grigorita Ko 5b, 25r, 30t; Tomas Kotouc 27b; Kungverylucky back cover, 6; Christopher P Mcleod 10; David Martinez Moreno 9b; Einar Muoni 24t; Ivanova N 15t; Nwdph 12;Otsphoto 28; Pakhnyushchy 26; Nathan Pang 19b; Ondrej Prosicky 8b, 13c, 25cl; Enrique Ramos 17b; Reikus 4; Slowmotiongli 17t; Adam Van Spronsen 14; stock_shot 27tl; Johan Swanepoel 11c; Mari Swanwpoel 29c; David TB 5tl; Alexi TM 15b; Topten22photo 21b; Anna Utekhina 20; ValSN 9t; Michael Verbeek 15c; Artem Verkhoglyad 18;Vladsilver 7c; John Michael Vosloo 16; Y F Wong 29t; Wynian 23cr; Jimmy Yan 19t.

Library and Achives Canada Cataloguing in Publication

Title: Building confidence / Honor Head.
Other titles: Anxiety and self-esteem
Names: Head, Honor, author.
Description: Series statement: Building resilience | Previously published under title: Anxiety and self-esteem. | Includes index.
Identifiers: Canadiana (print) 20200356631 | Canadiana (ebook) 20200356747
 ISBN 9781427128195 (hardcover) |
 ISBN 9781427128232 (softcover) |
 ISBN 9781427128270 (hardcover)
Subjects: LCSH: Confidence in children—Juvenile literature. |
 LCSH: Self-esteem in children—Juvenile literature. | LCSH: Anxiety in children—Juvenile literature. | LCSH: Stress management for children— Juvenile literature.
Classification: LCC BJ1533.C6 H43 2021 | DDC j155.4/191—dc23

Library of Congress Cataloging-in-Publication Data

Names: Head, Honor, author.
Title: Building confidence / Honor Head.
Description: New York : Crabtree Publishing Company, 2021. |
 Series: Building resilience | Includes index.
Identifiers: LCCN 2020045183 (print) | LCCN 2020045184 (ebook) |
 ISBN 9781427128195 (hardcover) |
 ISBN 9781427128232 (paperback) |
 ISBN 9781427128270 (ebook)
Subjects: LCSH: Self-esteem in children--Juvenile literature. | Self-perception-- Juvenile literature. | Stress management--Juvenile literature.
Classification: LCC BF723.S3 H43 2021 (print) | LCC BF723.S3 (ebook) |
 DDC 155.4/182--dc23
LC record available at https://lccn.loc.gov/2020045183
LC ebook record available at https://lccn.loc.gov/2020045184

Contents

Everyone faces challenging times in their life. This book will help you to develop the resilience skills you need to cope with difficult situations in all areas of life.

What does it mean to build resilience?

When we build resilience we can cope better with things, such as being bullied or losing a friend. Building resilience means we accept that times are difficult now, but that we can and will get back to enjoying life. Learning how to build resilience is a valuable life skill.

What is a trusted adult?

A trusted adult is anyone that you trust and who makes you feel safe. It can be a parent or caregiver, a relative, or a teacher. If you have no one you can to talk to, phone a helpline (see page 32).

What is anxiety?

Anxiety is feeling scared and worried because you don't know what might happen in the future. You could feel **anxious** about meeting new people. You could also feel anxious about being in the dark or trying something new.

Everyone feels anxious sometimes—even grown-ups.

Anxiety can make you very stressed, or worried. This can make you feel tired or sick.

Sometimes you can feel frightened and you do not know why. This might make it hard to sleep or give you bad dreams. These are signs of anxiety.

Anxiety can make you not want to do the things you used to enjoy. Talking to someone you trust about how you feel can help you feel better.

What is self-esteem?

Self-esteem is how you feel about yourself. High self-esteem is being happy about who you are. Low self-esteem is feeling that you are not good enough. It can make you think you cannot do anything right.

High self-esteem means you like who you are and enjoy being with other people.

To have high self-esteem does not mean you have to be perfect or good at everything. No one is perfect or good at everything.

As you grow up you will learn more about who you are. You will learn what you like to do. You will also learn there are things you are good at and things you are not so good at.

Being proud of who you are will help you build **resilience**. Resilience is the ability to bounce back when things go wrong. Think about the things you like about yourself. Can you make people laugh, or are you helpful at home?

Talk about it

It can be good to talk to a trusted adult when you feel anxious or scared. Talking is a great way to help you sort things out instead of keeping them bottled up. It can also make you feel you are understood and not alone.

You should not be **ashamed** of feeling angry, scared, or anxious. The best way to deal with these feelings is to talk to someone.

Choose a time to talk when your trusted adult is not too busy. Tell the adult you have something important to talk about. Saying that you need some quiet time together can help.

Talking about your feelings and fears is very grown up.

If you find it hard to talk, try drawing or writing down what is worrying you. This can help start the conversation. Often when you share a problem, it doesn't seem so frightening.

Have a plan

When people feel anxious it is often because they don't know what to expect or what is going to happen. It can help to talk to someone you trust. If you know what is making you anxious, explain it. Are you afraid something might happen?

It can help if you have a plan before you try something new or visit a new place.

Are you feeling anxious that a caregiver might forget you at school or the bus stop? This is something that may never happen. But being prepared can help calm your thoughts. Keep the name and contact information of someone you can call in case it does happen.

When you have a sleepover with a friend, arrange to call a parent or caregiver at a set time. If you feel upset, they can reassure you.

Having a plan makes you feel in control and this can help you feel less anxious. It helps to know you can do something about it.

Try new things

Trying new things is exciting, but sometimes you might worry that you will fail or not do something well enough. Sometimes people don't try new things because they don't want to **disappoint** family, friends, or teachers.

You will never know if you can do something until you try something new.

The most important thing is that you try things and do your best. Trying is more important than whether you get it right or not.

Be proud that you tried something new even if it didn't work out. Everyone gets things wrong, even grown-ups! This is part of learning to build resilience.

If you get something wrong, bounce back by trying again. Ask for help if you are not sure what to do. You are not a failure just because you cannot do something.

Build your confidence

It is normal for people to feel anxious when they think they may mess things up. **Confidence** is the feeling or belief that you can do something. When people lack confidence, they tend to doubt their abilities.

Instead of thinking things might go wrong, think about how well they might go.

To help build up your confidence, set some realistic goals. Make a list of things you would like to achieve, such as writing a poem, trying a new hobby, or keeping your room clean.

At the end of each day, think of all the good things you did that day. It can be helping with the chores at home or learning something at school. It can even be talking to a new classmate.

Praise others when they do things well. It makes us feel good when we make others feel happy.

Be yourself

Sometimes it feels bad if someone else is really good at something and you are not. It can make you feel like giving up. Don't get **discouraged**. You should not compare yourself with others.

Not all of us will be good at the same things.

Just because someone you know is really good at something, it doesn't mean you have to be good at it too. It would be very boring if we were all great at the same things.

Everyone has different things they are good at. Focus on what you are doing and be proud that you are doing it as well as you can.

Think about the things that you really love doing. Work toward being the best that you can be. For example, if you like swimming, try learning different strokes.

Control your worries

We need to learn to control our worries rather than letting our worries control us. When you start to worry, try doing something else to take your mind off the worry, such as reading a book or listening to music.

Try not to let worrying stop you from enjoying yourself and having fun.

Often when worries are written down, they don't look so bad. Write down or draw your worries and put them in a jar or a box with a lid.

Set aside a "worry time" of about 10 minutes every day. Try this about an hour before bedtime. Sit down with an adult, open the worry jar, and talk about the worries inside.

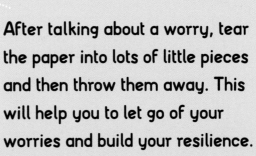

After talking about a worry, tear the paper into lots of little pieces and then throw them away. This will help you to let go of your worries and build your resilience.

19

Be an optimist

An optimist believes that good things will happen. If you are an optimist, you expect the best things to happen in any situation. For example, you believe you will make new friends, do well on your test, and win the game.

Optimists look forward to trying new things and meeting new people.

Being optimistic means that when you try something new you will feel less anxious about it.

If you are an optimist and something fails, you are more likely to bounce back or try again rather than give up.

At the end of each day, think of all the good and fun things that happened that day. Think of three things that you have to look forward to tomorrow.

Accept criticism

Criticism is when you are told you have done something wrong or not done something well. Criticism is something everyone experiences. Handling criticism is easier when you have confidence in yourself.

When someone criticizes you it is not because they think you are a bad person. Criticism should never be mean. It should help you to learn. You can use criticism to correct or improve your skills.

Criticism should be a good thing.

If you don't understand why someone is criticizing you, say so in a polite way. If criticism makes you feel anxious or stressed, talk to the person about how you feel.

If someone makes you feel embarrassed or hurt, it is a form of bullying. Tell someone you trust about it.

23

Make friends

Friends are very important. They can help us to feel good about ourselves. They are people we trust and can have fun with. Friends will also share our problems and help us when we feel anxious.

If you feel anxious about making friends, think of all the good things about yourself that would make you a nice friend.

Not everyone can get along. This does not mean there is a problem with you. It is just the way it is. You can't be friends with everyone.

24

Even if you can't be friends, be polite. You don't have to change who you are to fit in with other people.

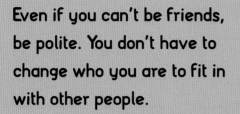

If your anxiety is stopping you from making new friends, talk to someone you trust about it. Don't feel **embarrassed**. Not everyone can make friends easily.

Eat right and exercise

Eating the right food, getting exercise, and having a good night's sleep can help make you feel less anxious. Good food and exercise give you the energy to deal with stress and anxiety.

Sleep helps your mind and body to feel happy and healthy.

Try not to eat too many sweet or fatty foods, such as candy and chips. These can make you feel tired, grumpy, and anxious.

You should eat to stay happy and healthy, not to change the way you look. If you can, eat fresh fruits and vegetables and drink lots of water.

Do some exercise every day. Look for fun games and sports to try, such as swimming or gymnastics.

Love being you

You are special. There is no one else like you in the whole world! Be proud of who you are, how you look, and the things that you do every day.

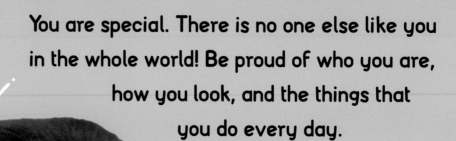

Be the best person you can be by being kind, polite, and honest. Enjoy being you!

We are all different shapes and sizes. Think about how amazing your body is and be proud of it.

Be yourself. If you start to think you want to look or be like someone else, stop. Instead, list all the things you like about yourself.

Choose friends who make you feel good about yourself and who are there for you, even when things go wrong. Good friends will help you build resilience.

Be resilient!

Being resilient means being able to cope when you feel sad or are going through a situation that makes you feel anxious. Here are some things you can do to boost your self-esteem and feel less worried.

- Start each day with a positive thought. Believe that today will be a good day.

- Take a few minutes to yourself and say something like: "I can do this" or "This will be all right." Take a deep breath and smile.

- Think about a time when you felt confident or proud of what you did. Remember how good you felt and try to keep feeling this way.

- When you feel anxious, your breathing becomes shallow. Breathe in deeply and count to three in your head. Then breathe out for a count of three. Do this until your breathing is normal or you start to feel better.

- Give your anxiety a name and a face. If you are anxious about meeting new people, think of how that worry would look as a person. When the worry starts, face it and tell it to go away and leave you alone.

Notes for parents, caregivers, and teachers

There are many ways parents, caregivers, and teachers can help children develop resilience skills through teaching them how to deal with their anxieties.

Children who lack confidence find it difficult to accept praise or criticism. They are reluctant to try new things, often have negative feelings about themselves, and give up easily.

Children with anxiety can develop phobias, be very clingy, or have separation issues. They may worry that bad things will happen to them, their family, or friends. Anxious children can be withdrawn, have panic attacks, and tantrums. They may also have stomachaches and trouble sleeping.

Never dismiss a child's anxiety or confidence issues as trivial. Try to get them to talk about how they feel and why they feel that way. At home or school, read through this book together. Talk about each scenario.

At school, have a safe, calm space where a child can go at a certain time to talk to someone about worrying or scary feelings, or just to sit and practice deep breathing.

Have a school assembly on anxiety and self-esteem. Be clear that these things are common and that everyone, even adults, feels this way at times.

At home, reassure your child that anxiety will pass. Acknowledge how they feel. Talk about it and it will seem less scary. Tell children you love them. Knowing they are loved unconditionally is a big factor in boosting resilience in children.

Encourage children with low self-confidence to try new things. Be clear that getting it wrong is not a bad thing. Praise their efforts. Help them to set goals. Talk about their achievements.

When a child does something wrong, look for positives rather than dwelling on the negatives. Encourage them to try again.

Glossary

anxious Feeling worried or scared about how something is going to turn out

ashamed Feeling embarrassed or guilty

confidence The belief that you can do something well

disappoint To not do as well as you or someone else hopes

discouraged Feeling let down or sad about something so that you don't want to do it again

embarrassed Feeling uncomfortable or shy

resilience Being able to bounce back from something stressful or bad that has happened to you

self-esteem The way you feel about yourself

Websites and helplines

If you need advice or someone to talk to, visit these websites or try these helplines.

www.boystown.org is an organization that helps children and youth in the United States. It has a helpline that has trained English and Spanish counselors working 24 hours a day, every day of the year. Call 1-800-448-3000.

www.kidshelpphone.ca has helpful information for children and youth in Canada. It has a helpline with trained English and French counselors. Call 1-800-668-6868.

www.mindyourmind.ca is a helpful website that gives tips on coping with issues and how to ask people for help.

Index